10 Things
for Kids to
Know About
POPE LEO XIV
I0820196

Imprimi Potest: Kevin Zubel, CSsR
Provincial, Denver Province
The Redemptorists

ISBN 978-0-7648-2910-9

Liguori Publications, a nonprofit corporation, is an apostolate of the Redemptorists. To learn more about the Redemptorists, visit Redemptorists.com.

To order, call 1-800-325-9521 or visit Liguori.org.

Printed in the United States of America

26 27 28 29 30 / 5 4 3 2 1

Written by Barbara Yoffie

Cover illustration: Ted Schluenderfritz
Interior illustrations: Ted Schluenderfritz, Shutterstock

Dear Parents and Guardians,

On May 8, 2025, Cardinal Robert Francis Prevost became the first pope from the United States. The 267th pope took the name Leo XIV.

Americans are excited to keep learning details about his life and are hopeful for the future of the Catholic Church. What do we know about Pope Leo XIV?

- His deep relationship with God and desire to live the gospel
- His American roots and knowledge of American history and culture
- His leadership roles in the Vatican and the Order of St. Augustine
- His missionary experience in Peru and compassion for the poor
- His academic background, including a doctorate in canon law

What should your child know about Pope Leo? You will find the answer to that question on the pages of this booklet, *10 Things for Kids to Know About Pope Leo XIV.*

The pages on the left side of this booklet tell a short story about Pope Leo's life, beginning with his birth in Chicago, Illinois, and concluding with his election as pope and introduction on the balcony of Saint Peter's Basilica. Children will discover facts about his family, his education, life as an Augustinian, his missionary work, and so much more!

Each activity page reinforces a key theme from the story page.

It is a fun way to help your child remember facts about Pope Leo's life. After you have finished all the activity pages, you can read his story over and over again!

1. His heart is full of love for God and for all people.

This is a story about a very kind and holy man.

His name is

The pope is the leader of the Catholic Church.

He teaches about the Catholic faith.

The pope celebrates Mass, prays for people, writes letters, gives speeches, and meets with leaders from around the world.

Pope Leo XIV's heart is full of love for God and for all the people in the world.

He wants everyone to respect each other and to live in peace.

Let's find out more about Pope Leo XIV!

What was he like before he became pope?

Color the picture.
What is your
favorite prayer?

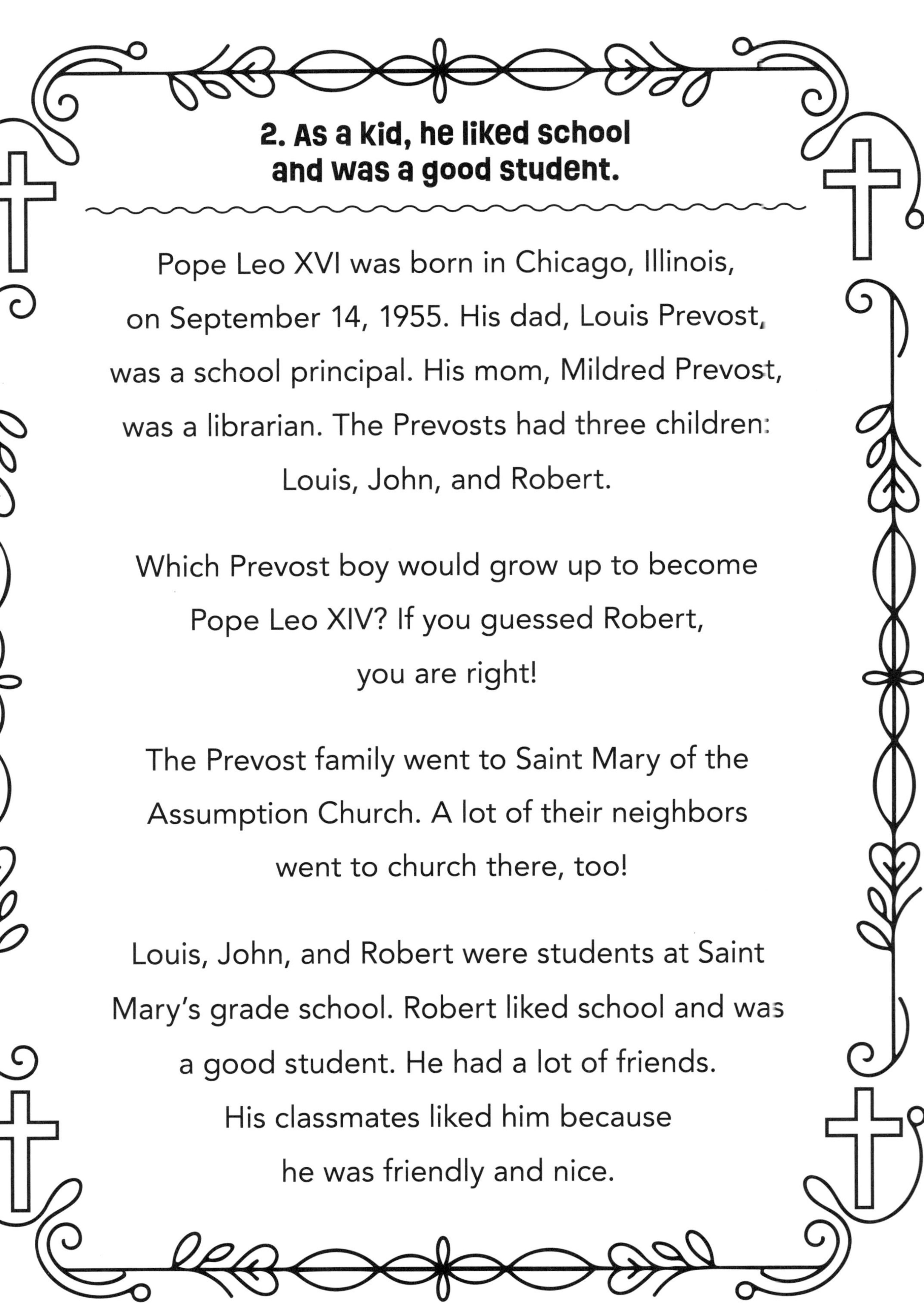

2. As a kid, he liked school and was a good student.

Pope Leo XVI was born in Chicago, Illinois, on September 14, 1955. His dad, Louis Prevost, was a school principal. His mom, Mildred Prevost, was a librarian. The Prevosts had three children: Louis, John, and Robert.

Which Prevost boy would grow up to become Pope Leo XIV? If you guessed Robert, you are right!

The Prevost family went to Saint Mary of the Assumption Church. A lot of their neighbors went to church there, too!

Louis, John, and Robert were students at Saint Mary's grade school. Robert liked school and was a good student. He had a lot of friends. His classmates liked him because he was friendly and nice.

The Prevost Family Tree

3. At an early age, he loved going to Mass and thought about becoming a priest.

The Prevost family liked to help out at their church.
The boys were altar servers.
Robert sang in the choir.
He loved going to Mass and often thought
about becoming a priest.
Robert pretended to say Mass at home
with his brothers!

After eighth grade,
Robert went to St. Augustine Seminary High School,
run by the Order of Saint Augustine.
This Order, or group of priests,
taught their students about the life
and teachings of St. Augustine.

Robert made new friends in high school.
His favorite activities were reading
and playing tennis.
He was president of his senior class.

Saint Augustine

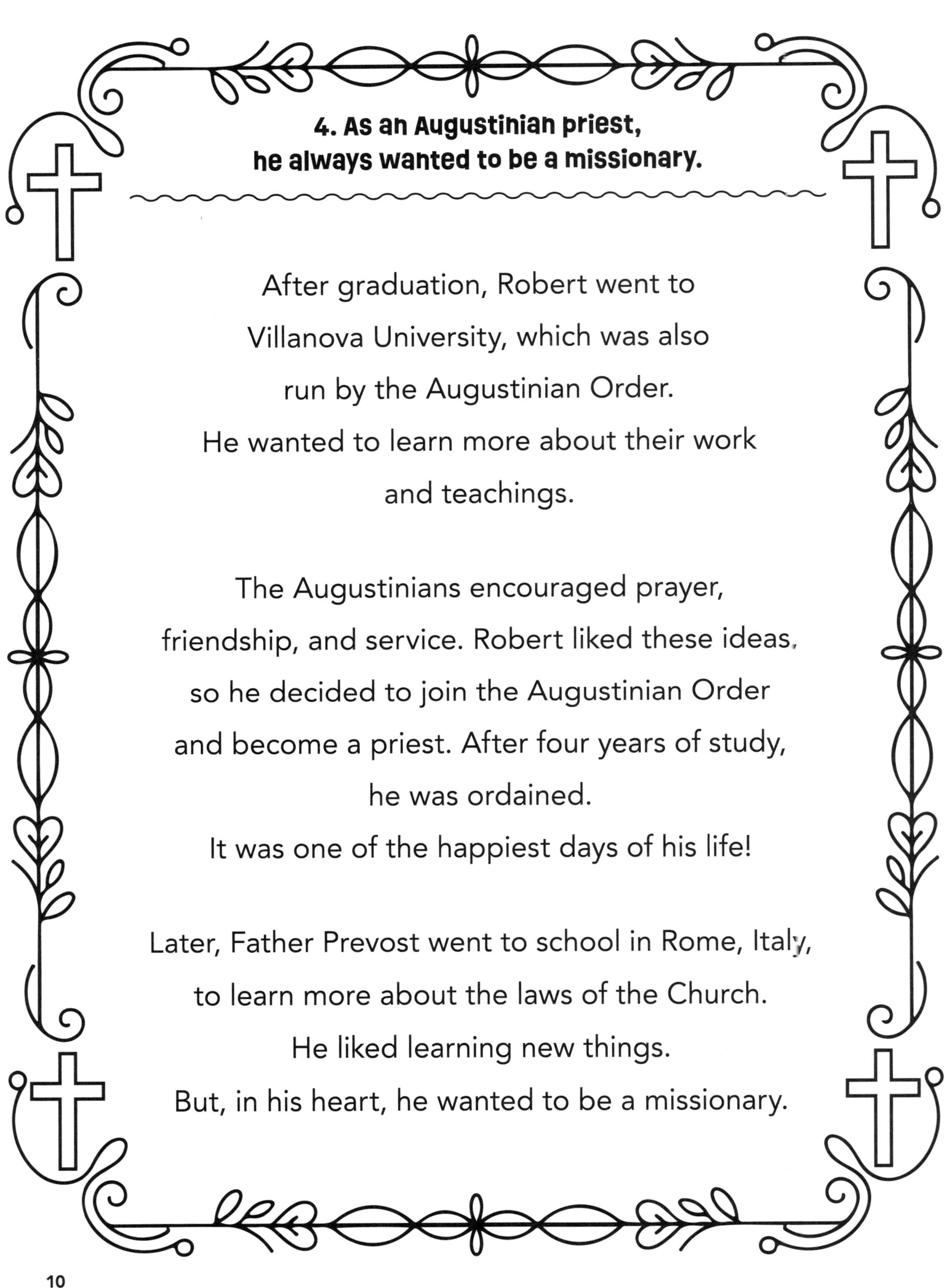

4. As an Augustinian priest, he always wanted to be a missionary.

After graduation, Robert went to Villanova University, which was also run by the Augustinian Order. He wanted to learn more about their work and teachings.

The Augustinians encouraged prayer, friendship, and service. Robert liked these ideas, so he decided to join the Augustinian Order and become a priest. After four years of study, he was ordained. It was one of the happiest days of his life!

Later, Father Prevost went to school in Rome, Italy, to learn more about the laws of the Church. He liked learning new things. But, in his heart, he wanted to be a missionary.

Use the words from the list below to fill in the blanks.

AUGUSTINIAN	VILLANOVA
CHURCH	PRIEST
FRIENDSHIP	GOD
PRAYER	MISSIONARY
ORDAINED	ITALY

A

C _ U _ _ H

G _ _

U

_ _ _ S _ _ N _ R _

P _ _ _ _ T

F _ I _ _ D _ _ _ P

O _ D _ _ N _ _

I _ _ L _

_ _ A _ _ R

V _ _ _ _ N _ V _

5. He was a holy missionary priest in Peru.

His prayers were answered!
Father Prevost was sent as a missionary
to the country of Peru in South America.
A missionary travels to another country
to teach people about God
and the Catholic faith.

He knew how to speak Spanish
and could talk to the people.
He became their friend.
The people called him Padre Roberto.
Padre means "father" in Spanish.

As a parish priest, Padre Roberto said Mass,
heard confessions,
and visited people in the small villages.
He also taught at the seminary
and trained young men to become priests.
He loved helping people.
He loved his missionary work in Peru.

How many hidden hearts can you find in the picture?

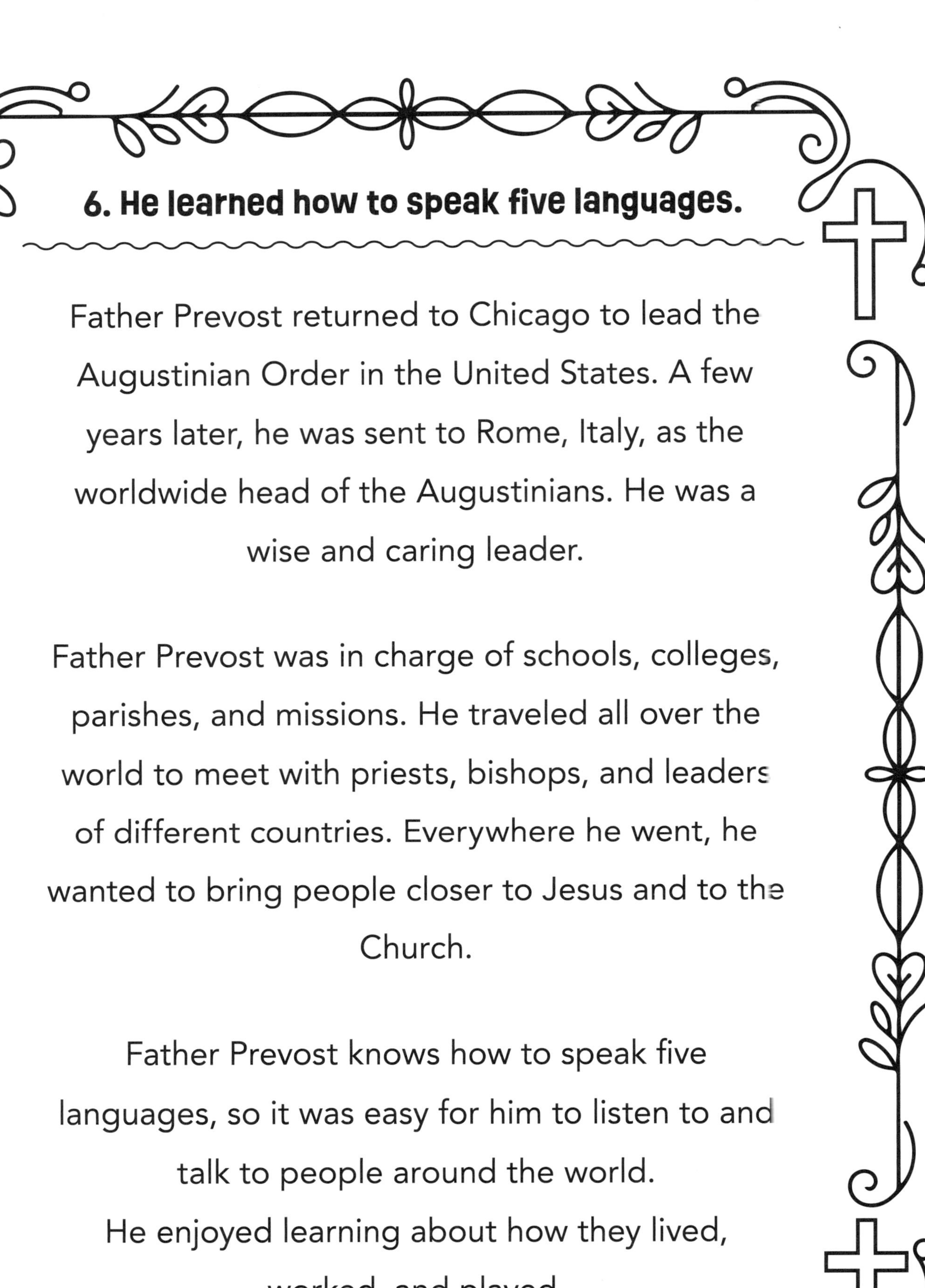

6. He learned how to speak five languages.

Father Prevost returned to Chicago to lead the Augustinian Order in the United States. A few years later, he was sent to Rome, Italy, as the worldwide head of the Augustinians. He was a wise and caring leader.

Father Prevost was in charge of schools, colleges, parishes, and missions. He traveled all over the world to meet with priests, bishops, and leaders of different countries. Everywhere he went, he wanted to bring people closer to Jesus and to the Church.

Father Prevost knows how to speak five languages, so it was easy for him to listen to and talk to people around the world.
He enjoyed learning about how they lived, worked, and played.

"Hello" in the five languages that Pope Leo speaks:

7. He became a citizen in two countries.

Father Prevost spent twelve years traveling to countries all over the world. But his heart was with the people of Peru. He prayed for them every day.

One morning, he received good news! Pope Francis was sending Father Prevost back to Peru to continue his missionary work. Pope Francis also made him a bishop. Now, he would be leading more priests and more churches.

Bishop Prevost was so happy living in Peru that he became a citizen, which meant he could live in Peru even though he had been born in the United States. Bishop Prevost had two homes: the United States and Peru!

Pope Leo XIV grew up in Chicago, Illinois. He became a missionary in Peru. Trace the line from Chicago to Peru. Color the flags and map.

Flag of the United States

Flag of Peru

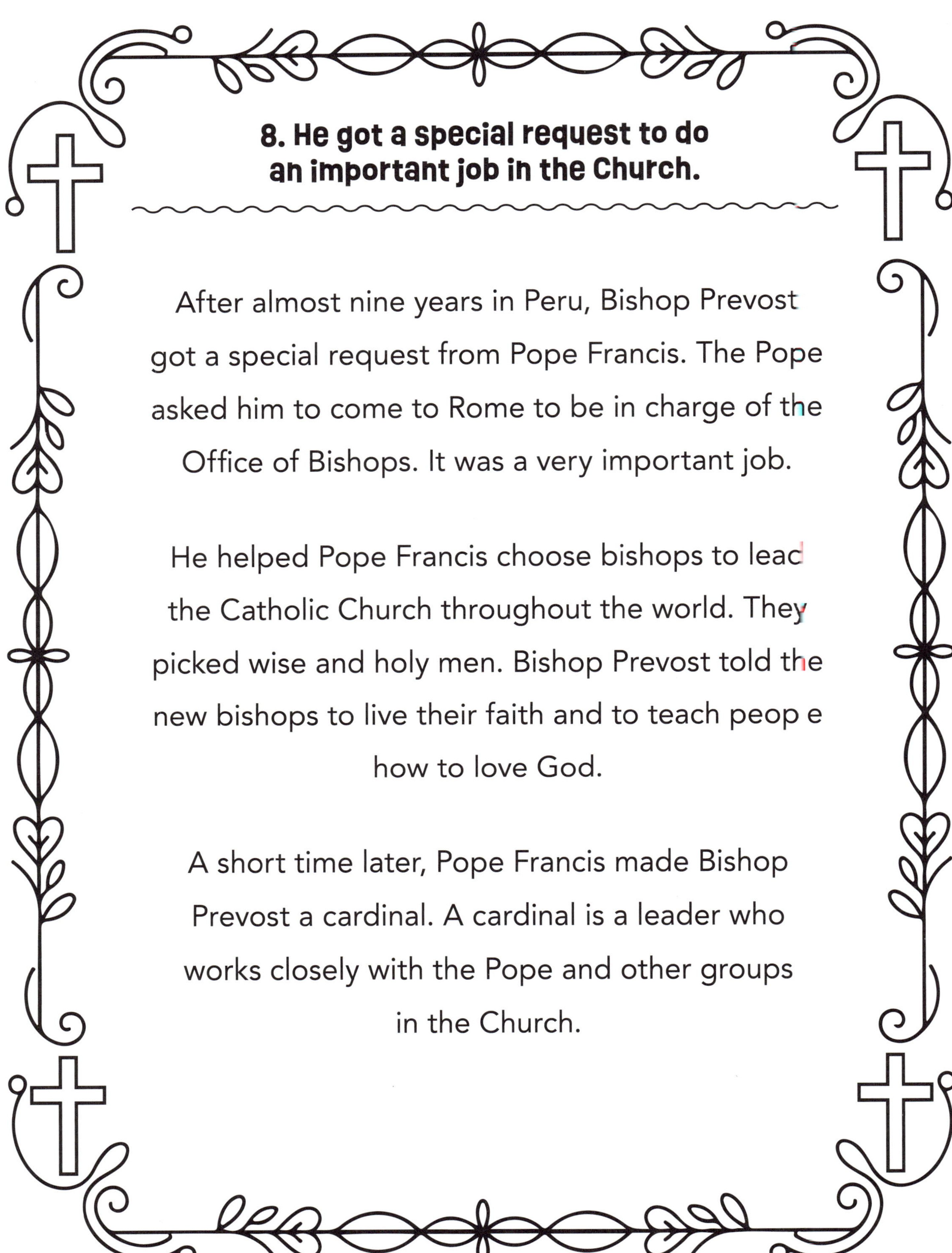

8. He got a special request to do an important job in the Church.

After almost nine years in Peru, Bishop Prevost got a special request from Pope Francis. The Pope asked him to come to Rome to be in charge of the Office of Bishops. It was a very important job.

He helped Pope Francis choose bishops to lead the Catholic Church throughout the world. They picked wise and holy men. Bishop Prevost told the new bishops to live their faith and to teach people how to love God.

A short time later, Pope Francis made Bishop Prevost a cardinal. A cardinal is a leader who works closely with the Pope and other groups in the Church.

Bishop to Cardinal Word Scramble

Unscramble the words.

1. ihspob ______________________________

2. lrnadica ______________________________

3. uhCcrh ______________________________

4. uePr ______________________________

5. poep ______________________________

Answers

Peru   bishop   cardinal   Church   pope

9. When elected as the pope, he trusted that it was God's plan.

Sadly, Pope Francis became very ill and died in 2025. Cardinals from all over the world came to Rome to choose a new pope. Cardinal Prevost was there, too.

The cardinals met in a large and beautiful chapel for an important meeting, called a *conclave*. They talked and prayed together. The cardinals asked the Holy Spirit to guide them. Who had the experience and the skills for the important job of pope? Who would become the new leader of the Catholic Church?

The cardinals voted. They chose Cardinal Robert Francis Prevost. Cardinal Prevost was surprised. He was also a little nervous. But he trusted that this was God's plan.

The Conclave Word Search

Circle the hidden words.

H	O	L	Y	S	P	I	R	I	T
C	I	U	O	C	H	A	P	E	L
O	K	V	K	Y	G	M	A	L	F
N	N	S	T	Y	P	P	D	W	G
C	T	G	E	N	O	R	Z	A	P
L	N	Z	L	F	P	Q	P	C	W
A	G	E	D	Q	E	O	J	U	O
V	O	K	R	B	F	L	D	L	J
E	D	R	N	M	Y	X	V	H	A
C	A	R	D	I	N	A	L	S	R

Word Key

POPE GOD CARDINALS CHAPEL

HOLY SPIRIT CONCLAVE

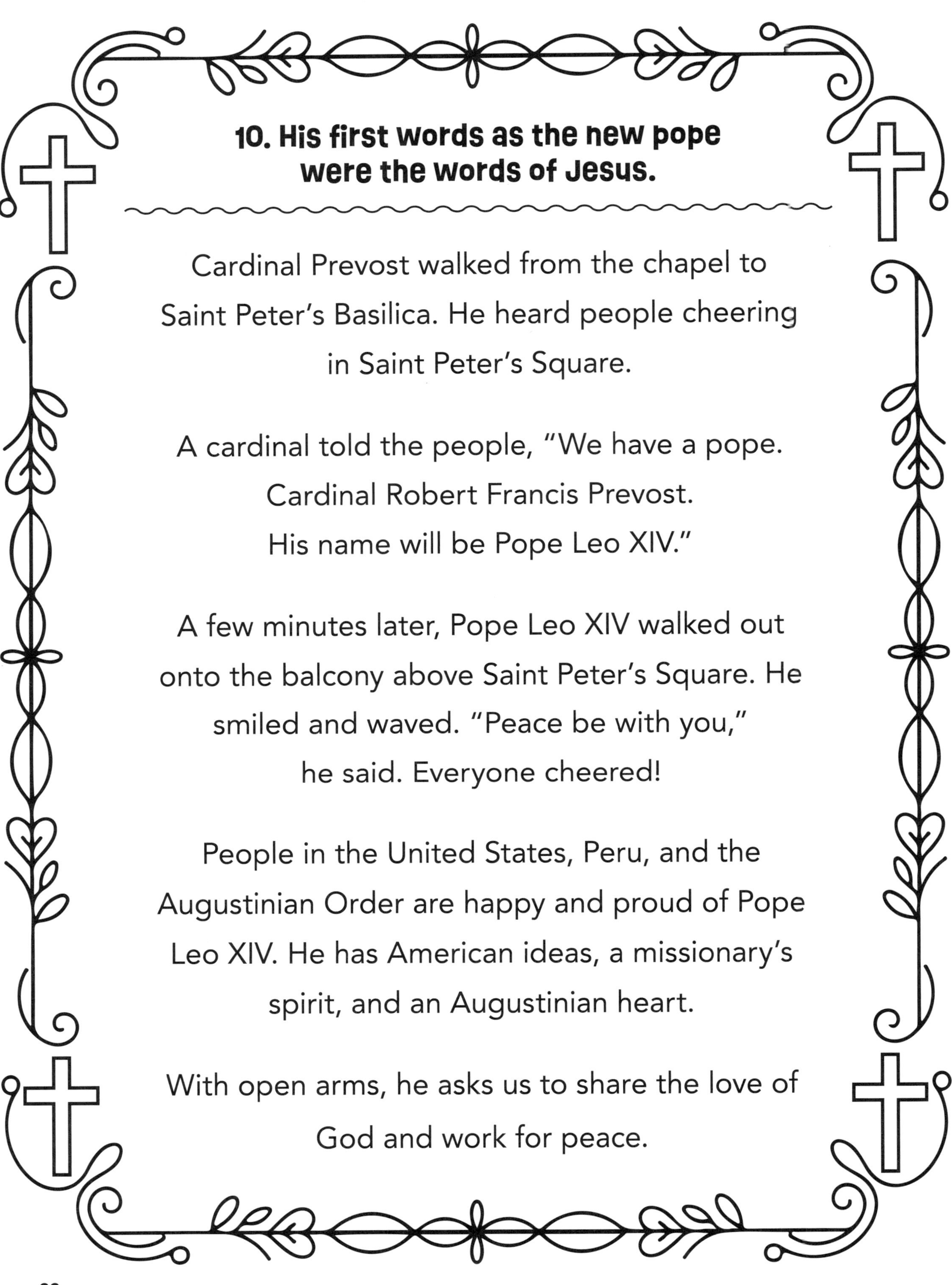

10. His first words as the new pope were the words of Jesus.

Cardinal Prevost walked from the chapel to Saint Peter's Basilica. He heard people cheering in Saint Peter's Square.

A cardinal told the people, "We have a pope. Cardinal Robert Francis Prevost. His name will be Pope Leo XIV."

A few minutes later, Pope Leo XIV walked out onto the balcony above Saint Peter's Square. He smiled and waved. "Peace be with you," he said. Everyone cheered!

People in the United States, Peru, and the Augustinian Order are happy and proud of Pope Leo XIV. He has American ideas, a missionary's spirit, and an Augustinian heart.

With open arms, he asks us to share the love of God and work for peace.

Peace be
with you.

On a separate piece of paper, write a letter to Pope Leo XIV. You can use the lines below to practice what you want to say.

Send your letter to:
His Holiness Pope Leo XIV
00120 Vatican City

Dear Jesus,
Thank you for choosing Pope Leo XIV to lead your Church.
Please help him do all the things that you would do.
And please help me be just like you, too!
Amen.